STRANGE HISTORIES
THE ROMANS

Fiona Macdonald

Belitha Press

LOOK FOR THE EMPEROR

Look for the emperor in boxes like this. Here you will find extra facts, stories and other interesting information about the strange world of the Romans.

▼ *Two Roman gladiators stand ready for battle, waiting for a signal from the referee. Before a fight, gladiators were honoured as heroes. Beautiful women tried to date them, and rich men sent fine gifts. But they did not live long to enjoy them!*

Produced by
Monkey Puzzle Media Ltd
Gissing's Farm, Fressingfield
Suffolk IP21 5SH, UK

First published in the UK in 2003 by
Belitha Press Limited
A member of Chrysalis Books plc
64 Brewery Road, London N7 9NT

Copyright © Belitha Press Ltd 2003

Designer: Jamie Asher
Editor: Kate Phelps
Picture Research: Lynda Lines

ISBN 1 84138 663 4

British Library Cataloguing in Publication Data for this book is available from the British Library.

Printed in Hong Kong
10 9 8 7 6 5 4 3 2 1

Acknowledgements
We wish to thank the following individuals and organizations for their help and assistance and for supplying material in their collections: AKG *back cover right* (Rabatti-Domingie), 2, 7 top (Pirozzi), 13 (Erich Lessing), 16 (Gilles Mermet), 17 top, 19 bottom, 20 (Erich Lessing); Ancient Art and Architecture Collection 4 (R Sheridan), 11 bottom (R Sheridan), 12 left (R Sheridan), 12 right, 23 middle; Art Archive *front cover* and *back cover left* (Museo Capitolino, Rome/Dagli Orti), 3 (Jan Vinchon Numismatist, Paris/Dagli Orti), 6 (Museo Della Civilta Romana, Rome/Dagli Orti), 10 (National Museum, Bucharest/Dagli Orti), 14 (Museo Prenestino Palestrina/Dagli Orti), 18 (Dagli Orti), 19 top (Archaelogical Museum, Madrid/Dagli Orti), 26 Archaeological Museum, Naples/Dagli Orti), 28 (Jan Vinchon Numismatist, Paris/Dagli Orti), 29; Corbis 22 (Roger Wood), 23 top (Bettmann), 23 bottom (Patrick Ward); C M Dixon 1, 5 top, 7 bottom, 8, 9 both, 11 top, 15 top, 17 bottom, 21 bottom, 24 both, 27; Robert Harding Picture Library 5 bottom; Topham Picturepoint 15 bottom; Werner Forman Archive 21 top, 25. Artwork by Michael Posen.

CONTENTS

▶ *Roman emperors used coins to advertise their achievements and remind conquered peoples of Roman power.*

MEET THE ROMANS

What were the Romans like? A strange mixture of nice and nasty, good and bad. They were brave, tough, hard-working and devoted to duty. But they could also be cruel, bloodthirsty, greedy and rude.

The Romans lived in Italy from about 753 BC to AD 476. Originally, their home was just one city, Rome. They grew stronger and took over other lands. Between around 100 BC and AD 200, they conquered one of the greatest empires the world has seen.

Everyone living in Roman lands had to pay Roman taxes and obey Roman laws. But they were not all equal.

▼ The Roman Empire was at its greatest around AD 117. It took people in Roman times over 100 days to travel across it from east to west, a distance of around 4000 km.

Roman Empire

London

EUROPE

Rome

Pompeii

Constantinople

AFRICA

◄ Roman soldiers and citizens. Today, many people still admire Roman achievements, such as roads, buildings, statues, poems and laws. But they think that some Roman customs – such as watching people kill each other for fun – were revolting.

FIRST CITIZENS

The Romans had a favourite legend that described how their city began. It said that the very first Romans were twin boys, called Romulus and Remus. They had been abandoned as babies and rescued by a friendly she-wolf. When the twins grew up, they decided to build a new city. Romulus became king and named the city after himself.

A few *patricians* (nobles) and *equites* (businessmen) were rich. Most ordinary people, called *plebeians*, were poor. Roman citizens – the people who lived in and around Rome – could vote. Non-citizens had fewer rights. But the biggest difference was between freeborn people and slaves. In law, slaves were like animals and could be beaten or starved by their owners.

▲ *Roman slaves were often painfully marked by signs of their slave status, such as brands (marks made with a red-hot iron) or tattoos.*

By around AD 100, about 54 000 000 men, women and children were ruled by Rome. They included Celts, Germans, Greeks, Africans, Egyptians and Jews. But it was hard to control and feed so many people, and to defend the empire's vast frontiers from invaders. In AD 476, the Roman government in Europe collapsed. Roman lands in the Middle East, became part of a new Byzantine Empire that lasted until 1453.

▶ *Rome was richer, prouder and more confident than any other city. The ruins of many of its fine buildings still survive today.*

ROMAN RULERS

The ruler of Rome was the most powerful man in the world. Many men and women wanted a share of that power. They were prepared to commit terrible crimes to get it. But often, their own lives ended violently.

At first, Rome was ruled by kings. The last was Tarquin the Proud. But Tarquin was very cruel as well as proud. On one occasion he murdered a king and then let his wife ride over the body in a chariot. He also made false accusations against some senators so that he could steal their wealth and their lands. He tried to make Rome's citizens obey him by bullying and terrorizing them. Eventually, the ordinary people plotted to get rid of him and he was thrown out in 509 BC.

EVIL KING

Tarquin the Proud seized power after his brother's wife persuaded him to kill her father (who was king), her husband (who was heir to the throne) and her sister (who was also Tarquin's wife)! Once they were all dead, Tarquin became king. She then married him and became queen.

◄ *Roman rulers were war-leaders as well as politicians. Here, a consul rides in a horse-drawn war chariot.*

A group of Roman senators. After Julius Caesar's death, his friends in the senate arranged for him to be honoured as a god. Failure to worship him was punishable by death!

▼ Emperor Augustus (who ruled from 27 BC to AD 14). Officially, he was just 'first citizen', but in fact he had total control. He reformed the government, and made many new laws – including one telling Romans to have more children.

Rome then became a republic (a state ruled by the people). It had two leaders, called consuls. The Romans thought this was safer than letting one man rule alone. New consuls were chosen every year by the Senate, an assembly of rich, powerful men.

In wartime, the Senate could ask one man to become dictator (all-powerful ruler) for a while. But this was risky, as the brilliant army commander Julius Caesar discovered in 44 BC. He was stabbed to death by his comrades, because they thought he was too fond of power.

After years of war and quarrelling, Caesar's great-nephew, Augustus, became emperor of Rome. Many emperors ruled after him, until AD 476. Some were mad (like Caligula, who made his horse a consul), and some were bad (like Nero, suspected of burning down half of Rome). But others were wise and ruled well.

THE ROMANS AT HOME

The size and the shape of a Roman house depended on how rich the owner was. Every Roman family dreamed of living in a *domus* (town house, built round a square courtyard garden) or a villa (large, elegant house in the country or by the sea).

But very few could afford a house like that. Most ordinary people had to rent a cheap home instead. In the country, poor families lived in wooden shacks with thatched roofs. They usually had a small garden plot, where they could keep chickens or a pig and grow vegetables. Poor people in towns lived in small, cramped apartments, with just one or two rooms, in rickety blocks of flats.

NO HOMES IN ROME

Homeless Romans found shelter where they could, in the doorways of temples and law courts, or under the covered walkways that surround city marketplaces. They kept a few belongings in baskets, which they chained to stone columns (part of all big Roman buildings) while they went to find food, or have a wash at the public baths.

▼ *With shops, workshops, warehouses and taverns at street level, Roman blocks of flats were noisy and often smelly places to live.*

A warm pool at the baths in the Roman city of Bath, England.
Most Roman homes had no bathrooms, lavatories or water supplies.
Poor families fetched water from street fountains, went to public lavatories (which had seats for several people, side by side!), and washed – once every nine days – at communal public baths.

Blocks of flats were known as *insulae* (islands), because each one was like a separate community. They had shops and taverns on the ground floor, and homeless people camping out on the roof! The best rooms were on the first floor. They had windows, which let in light and air, and balconies. The worst rooms were in the attic. These were dark, stuffy and damp.

Insulae were usually very badly built of timber and sun-dried mud, and they often fell down. They caught fire, too, because Roman people liked to keep warm by huddling round clay pots full of burning coals. Emperor Augustus tried to make blocks safer by limiting their height to 21m. He also set up a fire brigade run by slaves, but many people still died, trapped under rubble or in flames.

▼ A Roman villa in North Africa, surrounded by fields and farms – and some of the hundreds of slaves that worked there.

FAMILY LIFE

In Roman times, a family was more than just parents and children. It meant everyone else living under the same roof, including grandparents, aunts, uncles, cousins and slaves. It even included each family's own guardian spirits and ancestor gods, called *lares* and *genii*.

Romans were proud of their ancestors. They made wax masks of their dead faces and displayed them on their walls. The head of each family was the oldest living man, or *paterfamilias*. All family members were meant to obey him and honour him (and the spirits of dead ancestors who lived in him) with prayers on his birthday. In early Roman times, he had the power of life and death over the whole family, including his wife.

STRANGE REQUEST

Divorce was quite common in Roman times. Usually, a couple just chose to live apart, but sometimes divorces were arranged by families for political reasons. Cato was a famous Roman politician. His friend, Hortensius, wanted to marry a member of Cato's family, to show his support. So Hortensius asked Cato to divorce his own wife, so he could marry her. Amazingly, Cato agreed.

▶ *A Roman family, portrayed on a tombstone. All Romans relied on their families for support at home, at work, and even in politics.*

◄ A Roman betrothal (engagement) ring. Roman marriages were usually arranged by families, for political reasons or to help make business deals. Some husbands and wives loved one another; others got married to obey their parents or to please their families.

▼ Roman brides (right) wore a white dress, a yellow shawl and an orange veil. They were greeted by their new husbands with gifts of fire and water – signs of family strength and life.

Girls could marry when they were 12 years old; most men waited until they were around 20. Weddings were held in June, and wedding customs stayed the same for hundreds of years. The bride's hair was arranged – with a sharp pointed spear! – and she was dressed in a white wool tunic with a yellow cloak and flame-coloured veil and shoes.

Wedding guests came to her family home for a feast, where the bride and groom linked hands, shared food and watched while an offering was made to the gods. Then the bride was dragged from her mother's arms, taken to the groom's house and carried over the doorstep. This stopped her stumbling or falling as she entered her new home, which Romans thought would bring lifelong bad luck!

GROWING UP

Roman parents usually loved their children and treated them kindly. But most Romans did not want large families. Poor parents could not afford to feed lots of children, and rich families did not want to split up property between them.

A father had the power to decide whether babies born in his house should survive. A midwife laid each new baby at his feet. If he picked it up, it was welcomed into the family. If he did not, it was left outside on a manure heap. Childless women or slave-traders would visit the dumps every day, hoping to find a baby to adopt or to raise and sell.

◀ *A Roman child's toy soldier, made of baked clay.*

▲ *Roman babies were given a* bulla *(lucky charm, made of leather or metal) to wear around their necks. Girls kept this on until they got married; boys wore it until they were about 16.*

◄A Roman boy (centre) reads to a schoolmaster (left). A slave stands behind him, with his hand raised ready to beat him if he makes a mistake.

Rich boys went to school, where they learned reading, writing, maths and public speaking. Rich girls had lessons at home. They learned reading, writing, music, how to keep accounts and manage slaves. Although many families bought clothes from craft workshops, girls were also taught how to spin and weave. Even Emperor Augustus, the richest man in the world, insisted that his daughter wove all his clothes.

Poor boys and girls did not go to school. They had to work as soon as they were able, fetching water, running errands, looking after younger brothers and sisters or helping their parents in shops, workshops and farms.

CHILDREN'S NAMES

Roman girls were named on the eighth day after birth; boys one day later. Boys had two names, a personal one and a family one. Some had nicknames, too. But girls were just called by the female version of their family name. This meant that sisters' names were all the same. To avoid confusion, parents gave their daughters numbers – Prima (first), Secunda (Second), Tertia (Third) and so on.

FOOD AND DRINK

Few homes in ancient Rome had a kitchen. In towns, ordinary families bought takeaway food from shops and market stalls or ate snacks at bars. Country people cooked simple meals, such as barley porridge, in pots hung over an open fire. Most Romans, rich and poor, had only one hot meal a day.

The Roman Empire was huge and food varied from place to place. But generally, for breakfast, nearly everyone ate bread dipped in water, vinegar or diluted wine. For lunch, there was more bread, with a little cheese, olive oil, cold meat or fruit. Figs and grapes, eaten fresh or dried, were the cheapest, most plentiful fruits, but the Romans also enjoyed apples, pears, mulberries and dates.

▼ *A Roman banquet. The best chefs were superstars, like today.*

GREEDY GUESTS

During a feast, guests were entertained with music, singing and dancing or poetry-readings. They were encouraged to keep on eating, even if they were so full it made them sick. Some guests carried a feather with them to tickle their own throats and make themselves vomit more quickly.

The main meal of the day was *cena* (dinner), eaten late in the afternoon. Roman gardeners grew beans, lentils, beetroot, lettuce, cabbage, radishes and lots of onions and garlic. Everything was seasoned with the Romans' favourite sauce, called *garum*. It was made from fish innards, left for months to rot in the sun.

For rich families, dinner was a chance to display their wealth and impress important guests. They paid vast sums to skilled chefs to create sumptuous feasts. The ideal number of diners was nine. They stretched out on three couches, arranged around a low table. Slaves washed the guests' hands and feet, and gave them garlands of flowers to wear. Dinner party food was often very strange. Romans liked soft, fatty meats, such as calves' brains or sows' udders or milk-fed mice and snails. They enjoyed strong, spicy flavours, and foods in disguise – such as roast hare dressed up to look like a flying horse.

► Rich Romans ate from dishes made of fine pottery, silver and glass.

LOOKING GOOD

The clothes worn by Roman people were very simple – just a long rectangle of cloth, wrapped round the body to create either a tunic, a *toga* (cloak for men), a *stola* (trailing over-tunic, for women) or a *palla* (big shawl). They were held in place by belts, brooches and pins. Poor people used the same pieces of cloth as blankets at night.

Roman fashions changed over the years, especially for men. At first, all men wore togas (usually with nothing underneath). Then Greek-style tunics became popular, although priests, senators and lawyers still had togas for special occasions. Tunics were simpler to put on than togas, and much easier to move in. To keep warm, men wore cloaks of wool or leather, sometimes with a hood, or several tunics on top of each other.

MAKING FACES

Many Roman women – and some men – wore cosmetics made from powdered chalk, lead, lichen, stale wine and ashes. They cared for their skin with olive oil, milk – and ointments made of bird droppings. Often, these mixtures did more harm than good. Some were really poisonous.

◄ *Rich Roman women had slaves to help them dress, and to style their hair. Blonde was the most fashionable hair colour, even though most Romans had dark hair and brown eyes. So Roman soldiers captured blonde women in Germany, and cut off their hair to sell to make wigs.*

For parties, fashionable men might wear a matching set of loose, comfortable, brightly coloured robes, called a *synthesis*. They went to the barbers to have their hair and beards arranged in the latest style. Beards were popular before 300 BC and after around AD 100. Men also had all body hair plucked very painfully from their skin.

Roman women's clothes were similar to men's, but longer. Women and girls wore an ankle-length tunic with a stola on top and draped a palla around their shoulders. In company, many married women also covered their hair. Rich women's clothes often had coloured borders and could be trimmed with frills at the hem. Underneath, many women wore a wide band of soft cloth round the upper body, like a bra. For playing sports, women might wear something like a modern bikini (see page 18).

▲ *Wealthy women wore beautiful jewellery, made of gold, silver, precious stones and (as above) rare seashells.*

▶ *Roman cloth-merchants. Traditionally, Roman clothes were woven at home, from rough, cream-coloured wool. But rich Romans paid for robes made of Chinese silk and Indian cotton, dyed red and yellow with crushed earth, or purple with rotted shellfish. Men also paid for their woollen togas to be washed – in stale urine – and coated with fine clay. This gave them a shiny white finish.*

SPORTS AND LEISURE

The Romans liked holidays. Traditionally, every eighth day was a market day, when men and women dressed in their best and set out to do their shopping, visit their friends, play games or watch sport. Law courts and government offices were closed, and schoolchildren had the day off.

There were also many religious holidays throughout the year. Some lasted for almost a week. To relax at holiday times, Romans went to the baths, sports centres and theatres, watched dancers, mime-shows and acrobats, listened to music and poetry, or just walked and talked with friends.

Young men played team games similar to hockey and volleyball; lifted weights; rowed; ran races; threw the discus and javelin; boxed; wrestled and went swimming. Less active games, played by women as well as men, included draughts, dice and *tali* (like jacks played with the anklebones of sheep and goats).

▼ *This Roman mosaic shows young women keeping fit at a* palestra *(sports centre). They are playing with a ball.*

18

A fast and furious chariot-race. The Romans liked to bet on who would win. Supporters of rival teams cheered and shouted during races – and sometimes fought afterward, just like football fans today.

The most exciting Roman entertainment was chariot racing and gladiator fights. They were also the most dangerous. The biggest sports stadium was the Circus Maximus, with seats for 250 000 people. At the Circus, daring charioteers drove teams of horses seven times round a narrow course – a total distance of about 8 km. There were often crashes, when chariots overturned and horses and drivers were killed.

Gladiator fights were even more violent. Romans liked to see men fight and watch animals being killed for fun. Politicians and other powerful people sponsored shows and handed out free tickets, hoping the citizens would support them in return. Gladiators, who were usually slaves, prisoners of war or criminals, were treated like glamorous superstars. But their lives were short.

▼ *Gladiators fighting. In AD 108–109, Emperor Trajan paid for 117 days of fighting, to celebrate a great victory. Ten thousand gladiators took part, and 11 000 wild animals were killed.*

GODS AND FESTIVALS

Many different gods and goddesses were worshipped in ancient Rome. Some were borrowed from the Greeks, but had different names. Others were old Italian gods, or spirits who were thought to live in caves, rivers and trees. Everyone had to honour the spirits of dead and living emperors.

Each god or goddess looked after a different part of life. Jupiter was the most important. He was god of the sky and protector of the Roman state. Mars was the god of war, Venus was the goddess of love and Vesta was the goddess of fire. All the gods were served by priests and priestesses.

Roman people also looked for messages sent by the gods, especially before starting something important, like setting off on a journey or declaring war. Messages could be read in the weather, in mysterious events like eclipses and in animals.

Public prayers, sacrifices and processions were very important. They helped the Romans please the gods and ask for their help. But if anything went wrong, like a priest sneezing, then the ritual would be worthless.

▼ *Minerva was the goddess of wisdom. The Romans portrayed their gods and goddesses as superhumans – bigger, stronger and more beautiful than people.*

The Roman year was full of religious festivals. Work and government business was not allowed. Most festivals were full of fun, such as *Saturnalia*, in midwinter, when people gave presents, wore funny hats and played gambling games.

New gods, and strange ceremonies, came to Rome from conquered lands. Soldiers worshipped the Persian god Mithras with bull's blood, deep underground. Priests of the Syrian goddess Cybele whipped themselves into a frenzy, and danced through the streets.

▲ *Families prayed to lares (guardian spirits, centre) and penates (household gods, right and left) every day, and made offerings of incense and wine.*

GODS AND GODDESSES

The Romans worshipped many gods and goddesses. Here are some of them:

Jupiter – king of the gods
Juno – queen of the gods
Mars – god of war
Venus – goddess of love
Minerva – goddess of wisdom
Diana – goddess of hunting and the moon
Neptune – god of the sea
Mercury – messenger of the gods
Pluto – god of the underworld
Vesta – goddess of fire and the hearth
Vulcan – god of fire and volcanoes
Janus – god of doorways, beginnings and the new year.

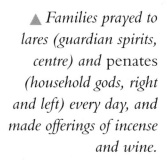

▶ *The Romans were very superstitious. They often consulted witches, who cast spells and curses, and made love potions from herbs – and dead bodies. This bronze hand is covered in magic charms.*

ROMANS AT WAR

The army made Rome great. Roman soldiers conquered new lands, defended the empire's frontiers and built splendid roads, walls, forts and camps. They spread Roman words, ideas, beliefs and customs wherever they went.

The Roman army was big, fit, well trained and disciplined. Between AD 100 and 200, when the empire was most powerful, it contained over 150 000 legionaries (citizen soldiers) and even more auxiliaries (soldiers recruited from friendly peoples in empire lands). Soldiers signed on for almost all their active adult life: legionaries had to serve for 20 years, auxiliaries for 25. They were well paid, but each man had to buy his own food.

◄ *A Roman mosaic showing soldiers fighting. Favourite Roman tactics were to march close to the enemy, then hurl javelins and spears. After that, they rushed forwards, crouching low to stab enemies in the stomach with short, sharp swords.*

Soldiers kept themselves fit and ready for battle by going on long marches (30 km a day), practising with their weapons and doing sports. They needed to be tough to survive a battle. Soldiers who fought bravely were rewarded with crowns of oak leaves or plaited grass – but they also hoped to get a share of loot from conquered enemies. A bold, lucky fighter might make his fortune this way.

Army discipline was ferocious. Men who ran away or disobeyed orders were killed. One commander even executed his own son. Savage punishments like 'decimation' forced soldiers to behave. If just one man in a cohort (unit of 500 soldiers) broke the rules, one in every ten was killed even though most of them had done nothing wrong. The men to die were chosen by lot.

▶ *This Roman soldier's helmet dates from around 4 BC.*

▶ *A short stabbing sword or dagger used by a Roman soldier.*

▼ *In hostile territory, Roman soldiers built strong forts and defensive barriers, like Hadrian's Wall, in north Britain.*

23

Sickness and Health

Although some people lived to be 100, most Romans died before they were 50 years old. The main causes of death were childbirth, injuries, accidents and infectious disease.

The Romans aimed to keep fit. The ideal was 'a healthy mind in a healthy body'. Men and boys were encouraged to take exercise, and public baths and lavatories helped everyone keep clean. Childhood was a very dangerous time. Only one in three Roman infants reached their fifth birthday.

► *The Romans prayed to the gods for healing, and left offerings in their temples, shaped like body parts, when they had been cured.*

◄ *A Roman doctor and his patients. At the back of this picture, you can see his surgical tools. You can also see a snake – the Roman symbol of magic healing.*

There were many doctors in Roman towns. There were also wise women, midwives and brutal army surgeons. None of them really understood the causes of disease, although they could set bones and ease some aches and pains with massage and herbal medicines. But many of their remedies were dangerous, and few could cure serious illnesses. So Roman people also consulted witches for magic cures and prayed to the gods for help.

Funerals were important. They honoured the dead, helped families cope with grief and stopped the dead person's spirit coming back as a spiteful ghost. Dead bodies were not allowed to stay in cities and towns, in case they spread disease. So they were carried out in solemn processions, accompanied by mourners wearing wax face masks of ancestors. Then they were buried alongside main roads, in stone coffins known as *sarcophagi*, meaning 'flesh-eaters'.

CURED BY CABBAGE?

Cabbage was one of the most popular plant remedies. It was crushed and spread on bruises and boils; stewed for headaches; fried in hot fat to treat sleeplessness; dried, powdered and sniffed to clear blocked noses; and squeezed to extract juice to use as ear drops.
(Do not try any of these.)

▼ *Roman tombs. The Romans believed that dead peoples' spirits went to Hades (the Underworld). They had to cross a dreadful river to get there. Mourners placed a coin in each dead person's mouth, to pay Charon, the ghostly ferryman.*

ROMAN FACTS

Here is a selection of interesting facts about the strange world of the Romans.

FOUNDING FARMERS

According to legend, Romulus began to build Rome in 753 BC. But archaeologists think the city is even older. They have found the remains of farmers' huts, dating from between 1000 and 800 BC. They think that these farmers, not Romulus or Remus, were probably the first citizens of Rome.

RIGHT NOT LEFT

Roman people thought that it was unlucky, or even wicked, to be left-handed. So they kept babies' left arms tied closely to their bodies for the first few months of life. They hoped that this would teach them to use their right hand.

SEWER THING

The Romans built an elaborate network of drains and sewers under their city. The largest, called the Cloaca Maxima, built around 300 BC, was so big that a horse and cart could drive along inside it. It is still in use today.

PET LOVERS

The Romans were very fond of pets, especially dogs. They had many different breeds, including huge wolfhounds for hunting and small, white, fluffy Maltese terriers. They also kept tame fish and monkeys, as well as pet birds which they taught to talk.

▼ *Fierce dogs guarded many Roman homes. Visitors were warned of them by mosaic pictures (below), plus the words 'Cave Canem' (beware of the dog).*

This modern model shows a Roman soldier using a device called a groma to make sure that the surface of a new road is level.

ROAD BUILDERS

There were over 85 000 km of roads throughout the Roman Empire. The Romans first built roads so soldiers could march quickly to fight against rebels. Later, they were used by merchants, travellers and government messengers who rode on fast horses.

LATIN SPEAKERS

The Romans spoke Latin. (Its name came from the region of Latium, in Italy.) Roman soldiers and government officials carried Latin all over the Roman Empire, and it became the language of scholars and the Roman Catholic Church for over 1000 years. Many modern European languages have developed from Latin, including Italian, Spanish, French, Romanian and Portuguese.

SPECIAL DAYS

Romans liked birthday presents and held birthday parties. They also celebrated Mother's Day. But this was not much fun for the house owner's wife. She had to give all the women slaves the day off and do their work herself.

TOP MATERIAL

The Romans invented concrete and used it in many big buildings. It was cheaper and stronger than stone.

NATIONAL STADIUM

The Colosseum, opened in AD 80, was the largest amphitheatre (public arena) in Rome. It was used to stage gladiator fights and mock sea-battles. It could seat at least 50 000 people, and had 80 separate entrances. Its walls were four tiers of stone and concrete arches. Cages for gladiators, prisoners and wild animals were hidden under the floor. Spectators were sheltered by a huge, moveable canvas roof operated by men hauling on ropes. The surface of the arena was thickly covered with sand – to soak up all the blood.

ROMAN WORDS

This glossary explains some of the words used in this book that you might not have seen before.

Auxiliaries
Soldiers recruited from friendly peoples in the Roman Empire. They were not Roman citizens.

Circus
Oval track, surrounded by seats, used for chariot races.

Citizen
A free man, living in Rome or nearby, who had the right to vote. After AD 212, all adult men living in the Roman Empire were made citizens.

Consul
Ruler of the Roman republic. Two consuls were elected each year.

Equites
Rich businessmen in Rome. (Originally, their name meant 'knights' or 'horsemen'.)

Dictator
Man who ruled alone, with total power.

Domus
Town house.

▲ *Fine gold and silver coins advertised Rome's wealth and splendour. They often had god-like portraits of emperors, and slogans praising them.*

Emperor
Ruler of the Roman Empire, after AD 27. The name means 'commander'.

Empire
Lands and peoples ruled by a foreign country.

Gladiator
Slave, criminal or (occasionally) volunteer who fought to entertain the public.

Legionaries

Soldiers who were Roman citizens. A legion contained between 5000 and 6000 soldiers. There were around 30 legions in the Roman army.

Midwife

Woman who helps a mother in childbirth.

Palla

Cloak or shawl worn by Roman women.

Patrician

Member of a Roman noble family.

Plebeian

An ordinary Roman man or woman.

Republic

A state ruled by its people.

Sacrifice

An offering to please the gods. These are often items of food and wine or animals.

Senate

An assembly of respected men who made laws and helped decide government policy in the Roman republic.

Stola

A floor-length over-tunic, worn by women.

Toga

A long, flowing robe, worn by Roman men and boys.

Villa

Country house, often very grand, comfortable and luxurious. Usually surrounded by farms worked by slaves.

▶ *The Romans liked seaside holidays. Rich families built villas along the beautiful Italian coast. All summer, they went boating, swimming or fishing, or relaxed in the warm sunshine.*

ROMAN PROJECTS

If you want to find out more about the Romans, here are some ideas for projects.

MAKE A ROMAN WRITING TABLET
Romans wrote letters and stories on long parchment scrolls. But they used little writing tablets, made of wood covered with wax, to make quick notes and rough jottings. They wrote on the wax with a stick called a *stylus*. One end was pointed for making marks in the wax. The other end was rounded for smoothing out mistakes.

You will need:
a small, shallow box with a lid; sticky tape;
heavy-duty sticky modelling clay (plasticine);
an empty ballpoint pen; a rolling pin.

1. Stick the bottom and the lid of the box together with tape along one of the long sides.
2. Roll out the modelling clay to fit neatly inside the box lid and bottom. It should be at least 1 cm thick.
3. Use the empty ballpoint to write in the modelling clay. Try writing some Roman words, such a *puer* (boy), *puella* (girl), *mater* (mother), *pater* (father), *magister* (teacher), *amicus* (male friend), *amica* (female friend).

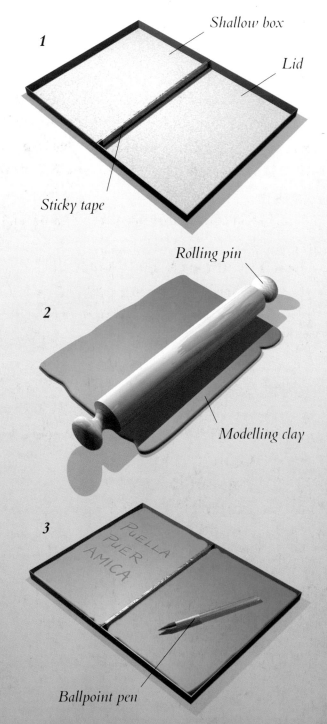

1   *Shallow box*   *Lid*   *Sticky tape*

2   *Rolling pin*   *Modelling clay*

3   *Ballpoint pen*

MAKE CARROTS IN SWEET-SOUR SAUCE

To make this Roman dish, you will need:

500g carrots, peeled and sliced into thin circles

15 ml spoon cooking oil

5 ml spoon ground cumin

5 ml spoon ground coriander

15 ml spoon honey OR soft brown sugar

15 ml spoon water

15 ml spoon vinegar

15 ml spoon currants, raisins or sultanas (optional)

5 ml spoon Thai fish sauce (tastes rather like Roman garum) OR good pinch each of salt and pepper

15 ml spoon chopped fresh parsley OR 5 ml spoon dried parsley

5 ml spoon cornflour/maize starch plus 15 ml spoon water

Ask an adult to help you.

1. Put carrots in a saucepan with lid. Add just enough water to cover them.
2. Boil carrots until tender (5–10 minutes).
3. To make the sauce, put oil, cumin and coriander into a separate small pan. Mix well, heat and let bubble for 2–3 minutes. Do not let the mixture burn.
4. Add honey OR sugar and water, and vinegar to the oil and spices in small pan. Stir well. Heat gently and keep on stirring until the honey or sugar is dissolved.
5. Carefully, bring sauce mixture to the boil. Let it bubble for 2–3 minutes, stirring all the time. Turn down the heat, and add Thai fish sauce OR salt and pepper, plus fresh OR dried parsley, and currants, raisins or sultanas, if using.
6. Bring to the boil again, then pour sauce mixture over carrots and their cooking water.
7. Mix cornflour with water. Add to carrots and sauce. Mix very well, then heat gently to boiling point, stirring all the time. Serve.

ROMANS ON THE INTERNET

Surfing the Internet is the quickest way to find out information about the Romans. But the Internet is constantly changing so if you can't find these websites try searching using the word 'Romans'.

http://members.aol.com/Donnclass/ Romelife.html
If you click on 'Great links' you will find many useful websites on ancient Rome.

http://historyforkids.org
Click on the picture of a Roman arch for a whole site on ancient Rome.

INDEX